MAKING UP LOST TIME

Poems by
David M. Adamson

Copyright ©David M. Adamson 2021

Photo 22812968 © Francis51 | Dreamstime.com

MAKING UP LOST TIME

Poems by
David M. Adamson

To Vickie, Richard, Victor, Jack, and Peggy
and so many
today and yesterday

Edenic Premises

"There's more than one way home."
--Keb' Mo'

Homecoming

I come back to sit at the kitchen window.
From here, nothing changes.
The curtains whiten in the sunlight.
The fruit trees dream in the still air.
The dog's bark rings to a rhythm
That beats on the pane and falls away.
The glass bluebird on the windowsill
Projects a tiny swimming pool on the white wall.
The grass grows longer, or shorter, or not at all.

Two young girls try to ride the dog, who's getting old.
The old woman claps her hands,
Then reaches on tiptoes for an apricot.
His bald spot sunburned, his house slippers muddy,
The old man points to me and laughs.
I tap on the window. They look away.
They know I'm watching.

The sun stays high and warm.
It flashes off the old man's glasses,
Giving birth to a light that fades,
A sentence that trails away.

Perhaps not changing is their way
Of sending for me.
Perhaps this is why I left.
So they would always be here.

Ascent

After the casseroles and the flowers,
and a last aging aunt blubbered goodbye,
we left the silent house,
drove up the canyon and climbed.
Astride one of your favorite trails,
we opened the urn
and gave your ashes to the Wasatch.
The light was changing as we descended
into the mountain's immense shadow.

Scattering Ashes

You can't summon the place or
remember how you got there
or picture the watching faces.

But you remember surprise
that human ashes are not powdery dust,
Apt to disintegrate like snow,
Or soft like bread cast upon the waters.

Dad's ashes chafed your palms like jagged seeds
As you clutched fistfuls from a plastic purple box
And flung them down a hillside
in Little Cottonwood Canyon.

And you remember urgency
As you retreated up the hill.

You had motions to go through,
space to occupy,
a black and white landscape to walk
among small figures filing along a dirt track
In the airless September heat.

Sleepwalker

Night-rise, sleep hums.
I wake and blow aboriginal dust from my lungs.
New citizen of silence,
I begin my search.
There's something I have to find.

My son sleeps like a chess master,
shocked into resignation.
His dreams of me are riddled with light,
luminous longing for a past.
Nocturnal naiveté.

My wife sleeps restlessly, still on the same side
of the half-empty bed, near the half-emptied closet.

Calm is all.
The furniture breathes quietly,
The dancers in the tapestry sway in the dark.
The house begins to shrink.

My breath settles onto bookshelves.
Pale light silvers the living room mirror.
My steps leave footprints before each foot falls.
The footprints lead back to my door.

Making Up Lost Time

It is time to lie down.
Adieu, adieu, adieu. Remember me.
I don't live here anymore.
My death has begun again.

Soon my son will awake
and begin to search
for things I left behind.

David M. Adamson

What You Left Behind
(for Jack Adamson)

The Shakespeare mug from which you gulped
gallons of instant Folger's,
ignoring omens from your gut.
An Olympia typewriter, emptied of words.
A brown wooden desk, a guilt-inducing self-indulgence.

The sprawling university where you gave
Donne's best light to their spheres,
and set Milton's myth moving
through the minds of rapt undergraduates
by the thousands
whose aging notebooks still inscribe
that poetry is the highest art,
for without it scripture cannot
utter the Word of God.

The "civilized diseases": headaches,
hemorrhoids, sinusitis,
high blood pressure,
that fissured your days
and drove you to the mountains.

The answer to "why climb a mountain"
and the rhythmic unity of body and mind
born from boots striding inclined trails.

Making Up Lost Time

A wife and children
who kept some of your memories as theirs.

An absence that became a maze
Where I circled for years in search
of something I could not name.

The wind from Emigration Canyon
that gathers in the cottonwoods
at dusk on a summer night.

Aspen trees filled with stars.
The deep shadow of the Wasatch against
the twilight sky.

But not the quest to seek and find.
Resting in peace would be eternal damnation.
Wander in restlessness, great soul.

Dream House

The red brick bungalow on University Street
set in a hill, faces west.
A boarded-up plate-glass window blinds it in one eye.
The damp gray cement steps
look worn by nostalgia.
The brass "61" still hangs, crooked above the porch.
This is where I began.
I stare at this house
that I haven't entered in 50 years.

It looks all wrong.
There should not be a maple tree near
the steps by the driveway
A box elder's missing from the parking strip.
The orange-berried pyracanthas
on either side of the steps have disappeared.
Roseate sunset light in the living room
has been swallowed by drowsy brick.
Days and nights of living noise
have seeped away.

Yet, ghost of myself,
I re-appear each night
to haunt this house
and mark its metamorphoses.

In a silent film, the 757 plunged itself into
this hillside in September 11, 2001.

Sucked into the insatiable future,
the house became cantilevered and glassed,
a red brick ziggurat
that extended across the valley to the desert.

Workmen built student condominiums,
department store workers report to work
a shopping mall,
an office tower,
a garden of lights,
a treehouse,
a sagging block of old businesses:
bookstore, barber shop, pharmacy, pizza house.

Most nights it becomes a house.
We live here.
We lament the lack of space,
at times from the new second floor,
at times enclosed in glass
to keep out mist and let in fading light.
Crickets whirr, rising and falling.
The dead welcome me back.
We overhear each other's whispers.

This brick double in front of me,
just right of daylight,
feels creased and sleepy.
It doesn't remember who I am.
And now I see it's only about half here.
The rest is memory and desire.

Night Falls on University Street

1.
We play kick the can
where the sidewalk cracks,
ruptured by a cottonwood's roots.
Then winds from the canyon rush
Through the tall cottonwoods
(I believed that sound was the sound
Of time roaring away),
and send us home.

I pause on the front porch.
From across the street a faint mist drifted,
Rain bird spray from Reservoir Park.
Chuff chuff chuff chuff.
At the horizon beyond the park,
jagged pink streaks taper into purplish dusk
above the shrinking mirror of Great Salt Lake.

2.
I enter the dark house
Things are not themselves.
Darkness billows from the living room couch.
Ink oozes from unlit lamps.
Shadows deform familiar shapes—
a chair, end table, a portrait, a piano,
driftwood from the Dead Sea—
into unnamed abstract dancing shades.

Making Up Lost Time

I watch my hands flicker,
merge into shade, dissolve
as I stand trying to grasp the darkness.

Soon car tires crunch on gravel,
a door opens, lights and voices soothe.
But I never forgot what the darkness did.

Lost Time

"We make our memories up anew every time we remember them."
— Felipe De Brigard

Tragic Pizza

The place smells the same. Garlic, undergraduate angst, oven flame. The menu hasn't changed. The Antony and Cleopatra. Italian sausage and snake meat. The Macbeth. Cooked in a cauldron. Red sauce stains. The Julius Caesar. Served bottom side up. You have to knife it from the back. The Timon of Athens. Bitter, ingredients, overcooked to black. The Frankenstein. Assembled from ingredients at hand. Served smoking from a jolt of high voltage. The Dramatic Irony. It's a surprise. Everyone at your table knows what you're getting. You cover your eyes.

You said tragedy means playing out a shitty hand. The game ends badly. Bigger Thomas. Joe Christmas. Hamlet. Everybody dies. No choices. The end. I said, no, it means you have a fatal flaw. Macbeth and Ted Kennedy—ruthless ambition. Gatsby—pride. Lear—vanity. Richard Nixon—paranoia, deep-fried.

"Can't be both," you said. "One is character, the other one's fate." "What if character is fate?" I asked smugly. "Then we're screwed, Heraclitus. It's late."

I smoked a pipe. You wore a beret and severely bobbed hair. I wrote sarcastic love letters to the universe. You wrote hate lyrics to Ted Hughes, love notes to Jane Eyre. We kept relations on an intellectual plane. You had a set of big firm ideas, dark-eyed principles, and a dimpled scorn of life's crap. My eloquence was tall, square-jawed, curly, tan. Together we solved the world's big problems as only undergraduates can.

"Can pizza be tragic; or is it merely postponed farce?" I wondered. "Here it is clearly both, though not at the same time," you said. "Does tragedy plus time equal comedy?" "Sounds right." "No, tragedy plus time is any order in this place on a Saturday night." After what seems like decades our orders arrive.

"What did you get?" I asked. "Looks like the double tragic," you replied. "Flawed choices and fate. I leave you without leaving a note. You were unfaithful to every love sonnet you ever wrote. Yet you are the first man who makes me feel loved, the only one who ever will. I strain for that feeling again and again. It becomes a boulder that keeps rolling back down the hill. And fate—my breasts that got so much attention from men will kill me. The only thing they will ever nurse is a cancerous seed. You?"

"The too-many-choices, done to perfection. Choosing everything means choosing nothing. Loving too many women, I love none. I follow a simple path home but try to stay lost. Living in the space between lost and found has a cost. My life becomes a solitary pilgrimage to no place."

"Let's not reduce our lives to a Harry Chapin song," we agreed. So we toasted the beauty of what never was. I went back to my hotel to write, found my way to a few easy truths, and called it a night.

Life and the Story of Life
for Richard

Today, leaves are falling.
"Aaron is watching the falling leaves."
The first day of school arrives.
"One day Champ's mom will take Aaron to school."

Life is the story of life, says the narrator.
Life expands. The story lengthens.
The intertwined threads begin to pull apart.

Life is surface and sheen,
laughter, tears, opaque signs.
The story strains after mythic frames,
the hero's prescience,
the villain's fall,
enduring love,
chimeric creatures beyond human sense.

Fable and magic
give form to stories
that we no longer star in.
New worlds take shape
where the story creates its own life,
an escape from the shock of recognition.

David M. Adamson

In time the threads converge again.
Life's pattern breaks and needs a new plot.
The stories yield their human meaning—
and lead us back to where we began,
where life is more than its story.
That is the story that must be told.

A Wanderer at the End

We are travelers all our lives.
Like the sun and moon, never come to rest.
When the body stops, the motion survives.

Time twists inside me. I buried two wives,
their love spent on an endless road. My quest
consumed them, traveling all their lives.

Profligate summer mocks my waning drives.
Riddles of the road languish here, unguessed,
where my body stops. The motion survives

in my art's vigor, you say, derives
force from what now seems the bitter jest
that we are travelers all our lives.

You, my friend, before the end arrives
there must be time to seek the west
beyond the sunset, where motion survives

in the dying sun, blazing, as it revives
inhuman tongues whose echoes, possessed,
sigh that we are travelers all our lives.
When the body stops, the motion survives.

Old Selves

Old selves die easily.
They whine their superseded demands
And the winds of change
Blow buildings down on them.

Or gasp their last
as the tub drains,
marooning them like bathtoys of despair.

One has expired in my arms.
His face turns to smoke
Like a ghost beginning to form.

Tenderly, I drag him to the backyard
To bury him with the others.
I unmark their graves
so oblivion knows where to find them.

Reclamation Project

Lie Down in Darkness
Stare toward blank heaven
discharging its dark.
Cue the poetry. Unquiet lines.
The past was worse
than you thought, its voices say.
Float toward sleep on a tide of loss and surface
into the empty skin of another day.

The Reappearing World
The border to the afterlife recrossed,
the dreamer is expelled from sleep, the dream lost.
I am the dream's shadow,
jagged with transition.
Light gathers me from every room
I have ever slept in.

Gloom is porous.
Things of the world resist
but return to radiance.
The world yawns.
A voice, laughter.
Love like laughter comes when it will.
Flecks of morning
dance in a square of sunlight.

David M. Adamson

Invocation

For Peggy, d. 1996 from Alzheimer's

    Absent spirit,
    soothe our hunger for consolation
    in the presence of this woman
    who asks for none.

    May the colored shapes we have become
    stand apart from these walls--
    where sun after sun has built
    a catacomb of days--
    distinctly enough to radiate love.

    Banish our loss.
    Dissolve the bitter mystery of why.
    Forgive the numb embrace
    We extend this slumping body
    Whose eyes reflect glass,
    Whose mind quests beyond this door
    Searching for a land of names.

    Give words to her passage,
    fled from our understanding.
    Resolve the twisted path she follows,
    the cratered wastes she speaks across,
    seeking kindred beings with cognate powers
    who name her as their own and exult.

Against Forgetting

My skin remembers your touch.
My calm remembers your care.
I loved once and was loved.
Read this to me when I'm not there.

Reasons for Watching the Sky

"Nature is a mutable cloud that is always and never the same."
--Emerson

1

The sky is not a barrier but a portal.
Pay attention.
It might be your only way out.

2

Farmers in a dry land
Watch for clouds.
Clouds promise rain.
Rain means food.
They learn from this
that chance falls from the sky
and fate grows from the ground.
This is the beginning of mystery.
They intone syllables
to a starry void.

3

Some who dream of infinity
believe a dark door
in the sky will open
and heaven will empty
and everything they have ever lost
will tumble back to them.

4

Through pinpricks in the night,
the desires of sleeping souls
rise into a second sky
where they flare into infinitude
like a longing for God.

5

In the garden hard with frost
sits an old man with furrowed eyes
staring at old decorations
dangling from branches
overhung with snow.

His forced breath sinks into fog.
He cannot feel
the rising of a warmer wind
or furrows beneath his feet
oozing life.

I am afraid of his eyes.
I turn away when he looks up
at waves of geese returning,
thawing the ground with their shadows.

6 Parousia

The others look at the ground.
They look at the sky.
They watch for a miracle,
Believing they believe,
Wondering when they will no longer wonder,
Unmusically quoting the New English Bible.

You ignore their designs.
You know there can only be moments
When we forget
The climate in our clothes
And the slaughter on our plates
And the tongues of our elders
And the mystery of what remains
And that light is our order
And our kingdom is stone
And that envy, joy, despair
Are rituals we cannot unlearn
As we touch and remember in predictable ways.

The sun burns a vicious circle.
You lie down to sleep.
You hope they remember to wake you.
But not too soon.

7 Eden

If you remade yourself,
this might be where you began.
The air is so dry that water dreams of rescue.
The sky settles into a viscous gray mosaic.
Beneath black fumes from a raging machine,
small objects can be heard to sigh.

A woman stares at the sky
as if trying to unsee creation.
A man's tongue sounds a rhythmic hiss a
That fails to become words.

People stream from the town square
after an indecipherable ritual—
perhaps a funeral for the sun.
They offer prayers for a new coveting.

Growing smaller and smaller
they begin a procession to the cemetery
to praise the bones of ancient myth
to please a peevish god.

This is our garden
in its ultracrepidarian disorder.
Our exile is desire,
longing for each new place of failure
between our beginning and ending
in vaster impurities.

8

Below a solitary cloud,
I feel its hunger for form.
It is trapped in its own becoming,
captive of chaos.

I am soothed by my confinement
inside the body's slower entropy.

9

The course of a cloud is not my course.
The sky's void is not my void.

The wind's not shifting in my direction.
Life is no longer up in the air.

The lines in my hand are a map.
All roads lead everywhere.

Today there is no walking away,
only walking.

10

Looking to the sky for transcendence
is the only course left.
Looking for submergence
denies our disconnection.
The ground is diseased.
The cure must be up there somewhere.

11

The blank sky tempts me
like an empty page.

Love and Other Arts

"Art and love are the same thing: The process of seeing yourself in things that are not you."
— Chuck Klosterman

Snowstorm

A man in a field walks through a storm.
Snowflakes on his eyelashes blur his vision.
A man in a study believes in snow,
In the truth of snow.

A man leaves traces as he walks.
His tracks ornament the field's blank.
He meanders, doubles back, evading,
leaves imprints that the snow erases.
A man walks. The snow falls.

In his study, a man devotes himself to snow.
He reads from the book of snow.
He composes wintry axioms.
"Snow: Atmospheric water vapor frozen into ice crystals
that drop on a walking man's eyelashes
or lie blank in an unwritten field."

"Snow is a conflict,
a confusion, a yearning.
Letters are desire.
Margins are melancholy."

The storm disappears.
A man peers at blurred words,
Resumes writing,
Shaking snow from the page.

David M. Adamson

Accidental Love Poem
For Vickie

A long time ago I tried to write
A love poem to a girl of my dreams.
I was burning and I was burning
For her. Instead, it seems

I wrote something about amnesia
And forgetting how to feel.
I wanted to win a dark mistress's heart
Only the burning was real.

Or a different story:
The gulf between objects and desire.
Like the soul in Emerson's tale,
We can never touch our beloved with fire.

Or loss. A long-legged beauty
Disappeared into echoes that I can't explain.
Still burning with thirst
I wrote about ashes and pain.

Then I met you on a blooming campus path.
You had sinewy curves and a powerful flame
In your eyes that left me burning
To give your pleasure a secret name.

But it turned into a different plot.
You told me I set something inside you free.
It was new and I was still learning.
I told you, "Come burn with me."

I think I know what the problem was.
I needed to learn a language from you,
The wordless speech that tongue teaches tongue,
Eye glints to eye, that skin lets through.

And our bodies coiled together
And your brown skin and my pale skin
Entangled in the heat of unity.
The burning flowed from the outside in.

There has to be a word for this,
Something enduring, strong.
Come close, I'll try to whisper it.
Though I might get it wrong.

Under Pale Starlight

In daylight she was a realist,
Anchored in a world of objects.
But under pale starlight,
Apparitions of his kisses
Danced across her skin

Desire for him, she told herself,
was a craving for form,
a way to fill the night
with soothing fiction.
But the truth was
she could no longer tell
love from addiction.

Photo Op

Patiently wait for the perfect light.
Glassy lake, wind, clouds, perfection feels near
as the moment dwindles into night.

Are flashes seized our only life, a height
of feeling between depths of time and fear
that our days are shades in imperfect light?

The moment missed is like a face out of sight
that against all logic we hope will appear
from around a corner, framed by the night.

Technology offers consolation in its sleight
of hand: Digitally correct the *here
and now,* counterfeit the perfect light.

Is there more than the remastered byte?
The flash between waiting and souvenir,
Fusing self and scene, reality felt right?

We wait for what's passing out of sight,
soft junction between soon and too late, sheer
threads connecting to the perfect light
before the moment dwindles into night.

Absence

Landscape with no transparent eyeball.
We are photographs.
Seeing is being.
Freeze fleeting things, filter clouds,
endless beauty a simple effect.

Funny how enclosures feel obsolete—
graves, houses, three-sided mornings—
when I am a share and share a like.
Like, like, like a googol of happy lives
better than yours.

I learned this fascinatin' (algo)rithm
from a sacred scroll:
It's reposts all the way down.

This is where we find ourselves,
saying yes to starting again,
absent this time.

Presence
For Vickie

Fiery light from a dying star
Cools against your mocha thigh.
Desire formed like fingers
Rustles your hair's dark light.

Body to body and breath to breath,
We are here and nowhere else.
Unposted selves,
Love without likes,
Hands without keyboards,
Voices in air,
The absence of absence.

Fleeting Things

A philosopher said, "Love fleeting things.
An angled shaft of sunlight piercing a mass
of clouds. A rainbow through dragonfly wings.
Water beads like shards of glass.

The fluttering shape of a sycamore's shade.
The sun sinking into its reflection
in a purple bay. Smoke's shadow. The rayed
curve of a finger reaching for perfection.

Whatever churns, bursts, rocks, flies,
foams, flickers, roils, evades,
in pigments of impermanent dyes,
enself it now before it fades.

Grieve the endless dying
of here and now, the present always past
elegized each moment, sighing
beauty is loss and can never last."

He got it wrong, in fact,
I learned from an artist's eye.
Beauty re-forms faster than we react,
faster than dreams dissolve and die.

Making Up Lost Time

Light coalesces into form,
form explodes into light
and we live lavishly inside this storm
if we learn to see it right.

Beauty multiplies, tapering, swelling;
Reshaping, reforming, familiar, then strange.
This gaudy blur in which we're dwelling,
This permanence of change.

Self-Portrait of an Artist

We revel in the artist's gaze.
See us, artist, we say.
Scale us in your geometry of sight.
Objectify us, break us down
to our vital light,
the zero shade of being,
essential black and white.

But what if figure becomes the ground?
Does the artist's vision ever come to rest?
Halt the eye's restless turning,
instead hunger to be seen? Fathomed? Expressed
in basic hues, simplified, resolved,
into the object deconstructed, mystery solved?

Spotlight and camouflage,
revelation and disguise:
The chiaroscuro of the artist's eye.
So where does beauty hide?
In us, beholders,
Invited in yet held outside?
Or in the starlight, sunlight,
Lamplight as it plays
On the seer seen in beauty's gaze?

To the Muse of Forgetting

"Forgetting is the purest form of clarity."
    —Someone

The unquiet dreams ended,
awkward reunions with the dead
traversing corridors of sleep,
stepping over the bodies of others' loss.
Ghosts gone from the gazebo.
No laments in the lowering sun.

She woke. Blue sky blinked into her eyes.
The room's climate began to clear.
The way from bed to door
became an upward winding stone path.

She climbed.
She stood in a garden with five black stones.
She foretold an eclipse,
burned the witch of winter.
She stepped in the same river twice.
She comforted her grandparents' bones.
She whispered a myth to god.

The sun shrank into the alarm clock's face.
Her breath brewed clouds above her head.
She sat aloof in the empty air,
Alone in the immense morning,
Resting in cold, clear perfection.

David M. Adamson

The Palace of Art

She invited me into her palace of art
where everything signified something else.
She wore a silvery gown with minuscule mirrors
that caught the light. I was not well-dressed.

I asked her to heal my jagged soul.
"My life is in fragments. Make me whole."

She already looked bored.
"I made this place to stand apart,
window to a purer world, deeply felt.
Everything here is for you. Take heart."

Music played.
Nirvana. Or maybe it was Deacon Blues.
Twisted letters carved
on doorknobs offered clues.

We followed a digital river
flowing beneath a winding stair
down to an analog sea.
I asked, "Are these 'caverns measureless to man'?"
"Yes," she said, "But not to woman."

We wandered through room after room,
One printed, one painted, one sculpted,
One paneled with friezes like the blazing tomb
of an epic queen deified by the sun.

Making Up Lost Time

I saw a room with a single chair.
The light defined its form,
its form leaked into light.
"Is this real or a photo?" I asked.
"Yes," she replied.

"What have you learned? So far I've revealed
that art is a shield against falling glass. Art healed
my divided mind, which used to devour
itself, giving away its power.

Art is hunger, a piercing lack.
Art is a ride on a gull's back.
Art is a dodge, the *as* of the mirror.
Art destroys, a callous clearer
of old orders. Art is a dance,
a surrender to chance.

Art is not all seduction and fire
or tethered to your desire.
Beyond the dazzle of you and me,
Art is failing light for learning how to see."

I said, "Now I understand less than before."
"Then you're ready, she said.
"Imagine starry ways beyond these walls.
Use an innocent eye. Confusion calls."

How to Use Poetry

1
To suspend
A summer day in glass.
Amiable green,
This blade of grass.

2
To give away
Grief, unfeel a caress,
Nourish a hunger
For emptiness.

3
To insinuate
to love's unanswered skin
syllables of desire
pricking in.

4
To build
a shelter of form
inside a chaos of weather,
a private storm.

5
To wander
through rooms of the mind
searching for enchanted objects.
What do I have to find?

6
To mark
against the slippage
of another year
that we were ever here.